TOASTS
for ALL
Occasions

TOASTS
for ALL
Occasions

By
Jeff and Deborah Herman

CAREER PRESS
3 Tice Road, P.O. Box 687
Franklin Lakes, NJ 07417
1-800-CAREER-1
201-848-0310 (NJ and outside U.S.)
Fax: 201-848-1727

TOASTS FOR ALL OCCASIONS

Cover design by Tom Phon Design

Printed in the U.S.A. by Book-mart Press

To order this title, please call toll-free 1-800-CAREER-1 (NJ and Canada: 201-848-0310) to order using VISA or MasterCard, or for further information on books from Career Press.

Library of Congress Cataloging-in-Publication Data

Herman, Jeff, 1958-
    Toasts for all occasions / by Jeff and Deborah Herman.
        p.   cm.
    Includes index.
    ISBN 1-56414-345-7 (pbk. : alk. Paper)
    1. Toasts.   I. Herman, Deborah, 1958-   II. Title.
PN6341.H47   1998
808.5'1--dc21   98-15774

DEDICATION

We dedicate this book to all those who know how to embrace the good things in life.

ACKNOWLEDGMENTS

So many of our favorite toasts were passed down from one happy reveler to another. We would love to acknowledge all of those gifted with the ability to create witticisms and sentimentalities special enough to be shared and concise enough to be remembered, so here is our general thank you. Thank you to those who have set up Internet chats or Web sites featuring your special poems and toasts. We want this book to reflect the language of our times as well as tradition. What better way than to glean up-to-the-minute contributions through the benefit of modern technology?

We would like to thank all the members of the National Speakers Association who took time out of their busy schedules to make wonderful contributions of advice and special toasts to our "Favorite Toasts from Favorite Hosts" chapter. They are: Ralph Archbold, Patricia Ball, Janelle Barlow, Frank Basile, Sheila Murray Bethel, Doc Blakely, Dianna Booher, Dave Broadfoot, Marjorie Brody, Dr. Gayle Carson, Steve Chandler, John Crudele, John Patrick Dolan, Art Fettig, Joyce Gibb, Richard Hadden, Keith Harrell, Cher Holton, Shep Hyken, Doug Jones, Brian Lee, Florence Littauer, Dennis McQuistion, W. Mitchell, Dr. Terry Paulson, Chuck Reeves, David A. Rich, Tim Richardson, Lee Robert, Dick Semaan, Jim Tunney, Al Walker, Somers White, Mikki Williams, Dave Yoho.

We would like to toast to a full recovery for Les Brown, an NSA member and inspirational speaker, who was unable to contribute to the book due to his battle with cancer.

Special thanks to NSA members and friends Danielle Kennedy and Jack Canfield, and to Michael Aun and Jeff Slutsky who shared toasts, advice, and excerpts from their wonderful book, *The Toastmasters Guide to Successful Speaking*.

Special, special thanks to Art Linkletter, a national treasure and a personal hero of Deborah's, who so graciously responded to our questionnaire in spite of his overwhelming commitments.

We greatly appreciate the efforts of Betsy Sheldon, Ron Fry, and the staff of Career Press for helping develop this project.

We could not have written this book without the help of friends and family members who contributed favorite stories and toasts, some not suitable to print. We would also like to thank our exceptional staff and spouses. Of course the spouses are us so we may as well acknowledge us with a toast: To a happy and wonderful life together filled with health and prosperity, which is what we wish for all of you.

CONTENTS

INTRODUCTION

When we began this project of compiling toasts for all occasions, we almost drove ourselves crazy looking for formal resources to provide us with definitive information on toasts and toast-giving. What we discovered was that toast-giving is a highly personal art. To give a toast is to honor someone you care about—or for whom you are publicly obligated to care. Whether at a wedding, birthday party, or gathering among friends, the right toast sets the mood for the evening's festivity and the memories to be taken from the moment.

A toast is the rare occasion when someone who could otherwise never say two words in front of a staring crowd is given the opportunity to take the spotlight. The good thing about a toast is that the spotlight may be on the toaster, but the attention should actually be paid to the toastee. If you are the type of person who freezes at the thought of being in front of a group of people and having to speak, this book will help you lighten up, enjoy yourself, and say something appropriate for the occasion.

As far as we can determine, toasts can be found as far back as this one, which was translated by Miguel Civil, of the Oriental Institute of the University of Chicago. According to studies, this is a 5,000-year-old toast that was given to a woman tavern keeper in ancient Mesopotamia:

Let the heart of the gakko vat be our heart!
What makes your heart feel wonderful,
Makes also our heart feel wonderful.
Our liver is happy, our heart is joyful.
You poured a libation over the brick of destiny,
You placed the foundations in peace and prosperity.
May Ninkasi live together with you!
Let her pour for you beer and wine,
Let the pouring of the sweet liquor resound pleasantly
for you!
In the reed buckets there is sweet beer,
I will make cupbearers, boys, and brewers stand by,
While I turn around the abundance of beer,
While I feel wonderful, I feel wonderful,
Drinking beer in a blissful mood,
Drinking liquor, feeling exhilarated,
With joy in the heart and a happy liver—
While my heart full of joy,
And my happy liver I covered with a garment fit for a
queen!

Although we are not completely convinced the Mesopotamians understood the consequences of a "happy liver," we know they understood how to join people together to honor someone important to them. There may be older toasts, but we are unable to locate one. Every known culture has had a tradition of celebration, so we feel it is safe to say that people were probably toasting to each other's health as far back as the lost city of Atlantis.

This book begins with "Favorite Toasts from Favorite Hosts." We were fortunate to receive many contributions from members of the National Speakers Association (NSA), an organization intended to enhance the level of professionalism among speakers in this country. We are very fortunate to be affiliated with this organization, and to know many of its fine members. Not only have they shared their personal favorites, they have given advice that should help even the most nervous and inexperienced toasters. Remember, you want your toast to be a good experience for you as well as for the honoree. If you heed the sage advice of the NSA speakers, you may find yourself on the road to a new career. You would be amazed at what happens to people when you put a microphone in their hands.

The rest of the book is broken down into categories of toasts. However, toasts often do not fit completely in one category or another. If you are looking for a toast for a particular occasion, you might want to look through all the chapters to find something you could modify to suit your needs. This is your chance to do something really original. For those few moments—and they should be brief—you can choose what to say and how to say it. We make no claims or representations that there won't be dire consequences if you say something tactless or inappropriate, but we can guarantee that originality and speaking from your heart are great places from which to begin.

Toasts are associated with joyous occasions. Humor, inspiration, and sentimentality are all welcome. Choose the type of toast that suits your personality most comfortably. If you can't find it here, make it up and let us know.

CHAPTER 1

FAVORITE TOASTS FROM FAVORITE HOSTS

The National Speakers Association is an organization dedicated to advancing the art and value of experts who speak professionally. Although we have never heard the term "professional toast-giver," these members of the National Speakers Association can guarantee that when people need someone to give a toast, they are often first on the list. Not only have they graciously shared their favorite toasts, they have shared their sage advice as to the do's and don'ts for the would-be toast-giver.

Ralph Archbold, a professional speaker who often portrays the historical character Benjamin Franklin, offers this perspective:

"We used to toast once to each of our 13 states. Now that we have 50, it could make for an interesting evening! I like one that goes:

> *Perpetual itching without benefit of scratching, to all of your enemies.*

"When giving a toast, make it short, make it pertain to the occasion and the people involved, and raise your glass high."

∾ ₰ ∾

Patricia Ball, author of *Straight Talk Is More Than Words*, shares this story:

"Mark Twain's *Diary of Adam and Eve* is part of the repertoire of memorable characters that I portray. At Eve's grave, Adam says, 'Wherever [Eve] was, there was Eden.' Upon the marriage of two close friends, I toasted the couple by telling the above story and then saying, 'Wherever they go, there is Eden.' "

∾ ₰ ∾

Joyce Gibb, author and visionary.

> *Pay no attention to what critics say. There has never been set up a statue in honor of a critic.*

∾ ₰ ∾

Michael Aun is the 1978 Toastmasters International World Champion Speaker, and author of four books, including *The Toastmaster's Guide to Successful Speaking*, *The Great Communicators*, *Marketing Masters*, and *Build a Better You, Starting Now!* He offers several toasts.

I could wish you good health,
I could wish you great wealth;
But your health could fail tomorrow,
And great wealth could bring deep sorrow.
So, I'll simply say, may God bless you!

Far better is to dare mighty things, to win glorious
triumphs, even though checkered by failure, than to take
rank with those poor spirits who neither enjoy much nor
suffer much, for they live in a gray twilight that knows
not victory nor defeat.
—Theodore Roosevelt

Do all the good you can, by all the means you can, in all
the ways you can, in all the places you can, to all the
people you can, as long as you can.
—John Wesley, English theologian

Do more than exist, live.
Do more than touch, feel.
Do more than look, observe.
Do more than read, absorb.
Do more than hear, listen.
Do more than think, ponder.
Do more than talk, say something.

"Have a list of books, like The Toastmaster's Guide to Successful Speaking on a suggested reading list. Be reasonable—in time, content, appropriateness, and humor. Nobody likes a bore. Say it quick and sit down. Two good things will happen: You'll keep it short, and they won't get bored. Both of these should yield excellent results for you."

∽ ❧ ∽

Janelle Barlow, co-author of *A Complaint is a Gift: Using Customer Feedback as a Strategic Tool*, says,

"I love toasts that let the audience learn something new about the person; and that gives better understanding of the celebrated person. Toast time is not complaint time—even if I believe complaints can be gifts. Toasts are a time for humor, praise, and congratulations."

∽ ❧ ∽

Sheila Murray Bethel, author of the best-selling book, *Making a Difference: 12 Qualities that Make You a Leader*, often uses a favorite Irish toast to honor friends:

May you live as long as you want, but never want as long as you live.

"Do some research for a timely and appropriate toast. They can be great."

∽ ❧ ∽

Frank Basile, professional speaker, author, and business executive, offers one of his favorites, an old Spanish toast.

> *"Amor, salud, dinero, y tiempo para gustarle—love, health, money, and time to enjoy it."*

∾ ༄ ∾

Dianna Booher, author of *Executive Portfolio of Model Speeches* and *Communicate with Confidence*, offers this wedding toast:

> *Marriage is a commitment to life. To the best two people can give to themselves and to each other. Marriage deepens and enriches every detail of living. Fun is more thrilling. Happiness is fuller. Compassion is stronger. Forgiveness is faster. Laughter is richer. Sharing is deeper. Marriage has more potential than any other relationship for bringing out the best in ourselves and living life to its fullest. May your marriage bind you closer than any other relationship on earth.*
> *(Toast #133 from* Executive Portfolio of Model Speeches, *Prentice Hall.)*

"Express your affection and good wishes for the individual. Focus on the other person, rather than yourself. Be brief."

∾ ༄ ∾

Dave Broadfoot, award winning speaker, writer, and comedian is founder and veteran of C.B.C. comedy, *Air Farce*; and star of hit TV special, *Dave Broadfoot: Old Enough to Say What I Want*. He's got two toasts he loves to use:

> *What's beautiful may not always be good, but what's good is always beautiful. Here's to what we are about to eat—it's really good!*
>
> *Nature gives us food, magic transforms it into exquisite cuisine. Here's to the magician!*

"Give your toast while you're still sober—coherence helps."

Doc Blakely is the author of *Doc Blakely's Handbook of Wit and Pungent Humor, Push-Button Wit, Keep 'Em Laughin'*, and others.

> *Here's to the desert*
> *And the valleys so green;*
> *Here's to the cowgirls*
> *And the cowboys so lean;*
> *Here's to the ones we love*
> *Dearest and most;*
> *And God bless Texas—*
> *That's a Texan's toast.*

"Never toast a man who is holding a gun; never toast a woman with fangs; and never toast any person who drinks from a sack."

Willie Jolley, author of the national bestseller, *It Only Takes a Minute to Change Your Life*, and host of the syndicated radio and television show, "The Magnificent Motivational Minute!"

> *My friend I wish health to you,*
> *I also wish wealth to you;*
> *I wish the best that life can give to you,*
> *And may dreams always come true to you.*
> *May fortune be kind to you,*
> *And happiness be true to you;*
> *And love be so sweet to you*
> *And life be long and good to you.*
> *And in this toast we give to you*
> *Our love we all give to you.*

"Make it brief, keep it short and sweet, make it simple and make it heartfelt."

ဟ ξ ဟ

Dr. Gayle Carson is the author of *How to Get to the Top and Stay There*:

> *My motto has always been "Be the best you can be,"*
> *...whatever that is.*

"Don't do anything so personal that it will embarrass the person involved, and always speak distinctly and loudly when you are giving the toast. (I have seen too many people mumble their way through [a toast], and no one can understand them.) Also, sometimes a private joke is too private, and no one gets it!"

ဟ ξ ဟ

Marjorie Brody is a professional speaker and seminar leader, and author of eight books, including *Speaking is an Audience-Centered Sport* and *Complete Business Etiquette Handbook*. She says:

"My favorite toasts have been ones I have given for good female friends at their *second* marriages. Each has been spontaneous (hence no script here). Included have been stories of their relationships, the fact that some people just don't get it right the first time, husband number-two has to try harder, etc. Although the toast is initially humorous, I end stressing the significance and joy of the occasion, and wish them well.

"If you want a polished presentation, prepare and practice the toast. Focus on three to five key points, then give examples. Although humor is effective, avoid jokes. Be careful you don't humiliate the receiver—slight embarrassment is okay, but say nothing they don't want the group to know about. Don't go on too long. Don't tell inside stories that the audience doesn't get. It's fine to make them hit the heart, and be emotional, but end in an upbeat spirit."

∾ ❧ ∾

Jack Canfield, co-author of *Chicken Soup for the Soul*, offers this contribution:

> *May you always work like you don't need the money;*
> *may you always love like you've never been hurt; and*
> *may you always dance like there's nobody watching.*

"Speak from your heart, and don't be afraid to be spontaneous."

∾ ❧ ∾

Steve Chandler, author or *100 Ways to Motivate Yourself*, suggests this familiar but nearly universally applicable toast:

> *God grant me the serenity to accept the things I cannot change,*
> *The courage to change the things I can change,*
> *And the wisdom to know the difference.*

"Make sure you have a minimum of six drinks before delivering your toast, so you're not too shy to make it moving and dramatic."

∾ ૐ ∾

Shep Hyken, professional speaker and author, suggests this toast for a wedding:

> *Live each day as if it's your last, and each night as if it*
> *was your first.*

"Be sincere and appropriate."

∾ ૐ ∾

John Patrick Dolan, attorney-at-law, professional speaker, NSA member, offers:

> *Here's to you and here's to me,*
> *And if we ever disagree,*
> *The heck with you! Here's to me!*

"Get to the point—short and sweet toasts are preferable to boring, long-winded diatribes."

∾ ૐ ∾

John Crudele, international presenter, author, and youth expert, reflects on drinking and toasting:

"One third of all adults in America over the age of 26 consume zero alcohol. I too host a alcohol-free life style, which I find affects the drink but not the toast.

"The tradition whereby someone is honored can be celebrated with everything from chilled milk or a frothed cappuccino, to a sparkling champagne substitute or frosty nonalcoholic beer. It's not the value of the drink that makes the memory, but rather the true feelings of sincere goodness in one's heart for another. Within the shared intimacies of the relationship, words of encouragement become liken to a prayer, as special meaning connects thoughts to hearts, and moments to lifetimes. Even the most mundane or trite becomes a celebration as friendships bond, invoking good will for one's future. A simple, spontaneous gesture and thoughtful reflection now lingers in the mind as time stands still in the busyness of our worlds.

"Next time, when the moment arises for the lifting of a glass, let not the alcohol distract from the spirit of your toast, nor the lack of alcohol the opportunity for souls to touch as tender memories are forever nurtured, shared, and savored."

ه‍ ‍.‍ه‍ ه‍

W. Mitchell, author, television host, and speaker, reveals a toast that John Wilson, a friend and former Navy SEAL, shared with him:

There are silver ships,
There are gold ships,
But there are no ships
Like friendships.

ه‍ ‍.‍ه‍ ه‍

Cher Holton, Ph.D., certified speaking professional, management consultant, and self-described impact consultant, says:

Here's to a recognition that it doesn't matter what great things you accomplish until you have inner peace; and once you have inner peace, it doesn't matter what great things you accomplish! May you have that inner peace throughout your life.

"Be enthusiastic, be sincere, and be short (in length, not height)!"

∼ ❧ ∼

Art Fettig, motivational humorist and author of *How to Hold an Audience in the Hollow of Your Hand,* offers three toasts:

May the road come up to meet you,
May the wind be always at your back,
And may the wind at your back never be your own,
Nor anyone else's.

To the Volunteer:

Give a cheer, give a cheer, for the Volunteer,
For while others say they'll see to it,
Give a cheer, give a cheer, for the Volunteer,
For they simply go out and do it.
Give a cheer, give a cheer, for the Volunteer,
They are brave, and they're ready for scrappin',
Give a cheer, give a cheer, for the Volunteer,
They're the people who make things happen.
Give a cheer, give a cheer, for the Volunteer,
I think God sends them down from above.
Give a cheer, give a cheer, for the Volunteer,
Yes, they fill this whole world full of love.

Toasts for All Occasions

A Toast to Seniors

Here's to the Seniors,
Survivors all.
Many answered
The Nation's call,

In the World War,
Korea too,
When fighting was
The thing to do.

You danced to Goodman
And T.D.
You made America
Strong and free.

You raised your kids
The best you could
In fact, you did
A world of good.

You worked, you sweat,
You did your share,
And now you wonder,
"Who's to care?"

Yes, here's to Seniors:
Let's give a cheer!
You get more loving
Year by year.

Richard Hadden, co-author of *Contented Cows Give Better Milk: The Plain Truth about Employee Reactions and Your Bottom Line* (Saltillo Press), notes,

"I am of Scottish ancestry, and my wife is a native Scot. The Scots probably invented the toast, and there are many Scottish and Gaelic toasts that we like. This first one is my personal favorite. It's called, 'There's Nae Luck Aboot the Hoose.'"

> *May the best ye've ever seen*
> *Be the worst ye'll ever see.*
> *May a moose ne'er leave your girnal*
> *Wi' a tear drap in his ee.*
> *May ye aye keep hale and hearty*
> *Till ye're auld enough tae dee,*
> *May ye aye be just as happy*
> *As I wish ye aye tae be.*
> *(Moose = mouse; girnal = pantry)*

"This is a popular Scottish toast that exudes the national pride of the Scots. It means something like, 'Here's to us; who else in the world is like the Scots? Not very many, and they're all dead anyway. What a shame!'"

> *Here's to us!*
> *Who's like us?*
> *Damn few, and they're all dead.*
> *More's the pity!*

∾ ફ઼ ∾

> *Lang may your lum reek...*
> *W' other folks coal.*
> *(Lum = chimney, reek = smoke)*

∾ ફ઼ ∾

"The following toast, called "The Toast Master's Companion," was first uttered in Stirling, Scotland, in 1822. It gives some insight into what was important in that day and place. It works as well in the U.S. as then in Scotland."

May opinion never float on the waves of ignorance,
May we look forward with pleasure, and backwards
without remorse,
May we never crack a joke to break a reputation,
May we never suffer for principles we do not hold,
May we live to learn, and learn to live well,
May we live in pleasure and die out of debt,
A head to earn and a heart to spend,
Health of body, peace of mind, a clean shirt and a
guinea*.
(A guinea was one pound, one shilling—a little less
than $2.)

ᴏᴡ ʃᴀ ᴏᴡ

I drink to the health of another,
And the drink I drink to is he,
In the hope that he drinks to another,
And the other he drinks to is me.

"Make the toast while you're sober; know the toast by heart well enough to speak it perfectly even if you're not sober; and if you make up your own toast, keep it short."

ᴏᴡ ʃᴀ ᴏᴡ

Keith Harrell, President and CEO of Harrell Performance Systems, and author of *Attitude is Everything*©, remembers his favorite toast given at a friend's wedding.

"The best man stood up and asked everyone else to stand. He then sat down and raised his glass in the air saying:

> *I am sitting down because I wanted to look up to the happiness, to the love, and to the joy this moment brings us all. We toast to wonderful people, wonderful friends, and I pray that the joy we all feel at the present moment will outlast us all.*

"If you're not naturally funny, don't try to be. Be sincere."

ᴄᴡ ꜰᴀ ᴄᴡ

Doug Jones is an international speaker and seminar leader on sales and sales management.

> *Hope for the best,*
> *Expect the worst;*
> *Life is a play,*
> *And we're unrehearsed!*

"Remember for whom you toast: Direct your comments to that person primarily, while acknowledging the others secondarily...and deliver *slowly*!"

ᴄᴡ ꜰᴀ ᴄᴡ

Danielle Kennedy, author of *Seven-Figure Selling* (Berkeley, 1996), comments:

"Being a good Irish girl, this is a favorite of mine. It makes me and everyone else feel special and loved.

Old Irish Blessing

May the road rise up to meet you,
May the wind be always at your back,
May the sun shine warm upon your face,
And until we meet again,
May God hold you in the hollow of his hand.

Don't get sloppy. If you feel so inclined, have your understudy do the honors."

ⱷ ⸙ ⱷ

Dennis McQuistion, author, speaker, and PBS talk show host, contributes a toast that he says is used mostly for birthdays, and has just the slightest sexual innuendo, which makes it somewhat titillating when guests are slightly inebriated, or about to be.

May you live as long as you want to,
And want to as long as you live.

"Be enthusiastic. Be unique and personal (unlike the above)."

ⱷ ⸙ ⱷ

Brian Lee, professional speaker and author of *The Wedding M.C.*, offers this outline for a perfect toast to the bride:

1. Introduce your toast. "Mr./Madame Master of Ceremonies, Head Table Guests, Ladies and Gentlemen, and especially (Bride's first name)."

2. Explain relationship between you and the bride.

3. Share two or three personal humorous anecdotes involving the bride growing up, dating, working, etc. (don't overly embarrass).

4. Point out a few of the bride's achievements, better qualities. Flatter her.

5. Perhaps offer a few words of advice to the groom on how to get along with the bride.

6. Wish her and the groom success and happiness.

7. Add any other appropriate comments.

8. Properly lead guests through the toasting:

   'Ladies and Gentlemen, would you please stand (pause until they do) and raise your glasses to the bride.'

"Above all, be certain to say, 'Ladies and Gentlemen, please raise your glasses (wait until they do) in a toast to (person's name).' Audience will follow your lead as you sip from your glass."

∼ ❧ ∼

Art Linkletter is author of 26 books, and star of two of the longest running shows in TV/radio history, *People are Funny* (19 years) and *House Party* (26 years). He comments,

"My favorite toasts have changed through my career. Looking back, I now note that my toasts as a young man seemed 'smart-alecky' (and occasionally naughty). As a middle-aged man, they were more inspirational, and now as a senior citizen, my taste is toward the sentimental. A toast I use often, at gatherings of people over the age of 50, concerns friendship, since in our later years I find that family and friends are the greatest source of happiness.

Here's to Friendship

Make new friends, but keep the old;
Those are silver, these are gold.
New-made friends, like new wine,
Age will mellow and refine.
Brow may furrow, hair turn gray,
But friendship never knows decay;
For 'mid old friends, tried and true,
We once again our youth renew.
So cherish friendship in your breast;
New is good, but old is best.
Make new friends, but keep the old;
Those are silver, these are gold.

"Think carefully about where you will be giving your toast, and to whom. Some toasts can be roasts, providing there's no cruelty to the humor. There's no reason ever to hurt anyone, or offend them by the material you have selected."

Florence Littauer, award winning speaker and author of 25 books, including *Personality Plus* and *Silver Boxes: The Gift of Encouragement,* says:

"My favorite toasts are ones that are uplifting, light-hearted, positive, and have a rhyme. Here is a sample toast that I gave to my friend Bill Peterson at the CBA Baker-Revell Dinner:

A Vessel for Noble Purposes

There are vessels for noble purposes,
Some for common use each day,
Some are of gold or silver,
Some are of wood or clay.
Some are fashioned from the mud,
Some pulled up from the mire,
Some have been perfected
Through the refiner's fire.

Bill has lived in such a way
That we can hear his potter say,
"I am so pleased with this lump of clay
Who's become perfected along the way,
Who's done so much for CBA."
So for Baker Books, and all of us here today,
We thank you, Bill, for coming our way.

Be positive, lighthearted, complimentary, and encouraging. Use the words to build the person up. Use humor that is in good taste (not slanderous, sexual, or discriminatory). Avoid sarcasm, because that usually emphasizes the person's faults and humiliates him/her. Evaluate what will be said and make sure it will not hurt the person's feelings or be a disparaging remark.

∽ ⁂ ∽

Dr. Terry Paulson, psychologist, provides practical and entertaining programs on managing oneself and leading others through change. He frequently uses the traditional Irish blessing (variations are included on pages 25 and 30.) Here, he shows two other favorites:

A Wedding Toast for My Son and Daughter-in-Law:

One and all, lift your glasses.
Here is to the bride and groom:
To your long health, to shared laughter,
To the magical and meaningful memories
You will create together.
To the wings of love
That will let you soar even higher together
Through the peaks and valleys life provides.
Here is to the twinkle of love in your eyes
That reminds each of us of our love renewed.
May God bless you and keep you.
God-willing, may you live as long as you want to
And want to as long as you live.
And for this one day, may your worn out smile muscles
Not cramp your lips so much you can't kiss tonight.
With this toast, as a community of friends and family,
We pledge our ongoing support and prayers.

Short Wedding Toast
To you both:
May the most you hope for
Be the least you receive.
May you live all the days of your life together.

ﾃ ｊﾃ

Chuck Reaves, professional moderator, and frequent moderator and emcee for clients all over the world, offers some sound toasting advice:

"First of all, focus on the person being toasted. This is not about you, this is about them. If you do this, you will find yourself less nervous (because you will realize that the attention is on the recipient and not you) and you will be more sincere. Instead of making a presentation, you will be making a personal statement or tribute.

"Next, be yourself. What has worked for others may not work for you. If you are a naturally funny person, use humor. If humor does not come easily to you, it probably won't work well in a toast. When the humor fails, the attention is on the person making the toast, not the one being toasted. Use your vocabulary, your accent, and your natural style to make the toast. In all likelihood, your toast will not be on the evening news, so don't worry about being 'professional.'

"Finally, ask yourself, 'If this toast were given for me, how would I feel?' If you would feel warm, humbled, honored, etc., it is probably a good toast. If you would be embarrassed, intimidated, or thinking, 'Gee, I wish my parents weren't here...,' then it's probably not a good one."

ოა ჶა ოა

Tim Richardson, presenter of outdoor learning and mind-stretching seminars for Personal and Professional Growth, remembers,

"My most memorable toast started with, 'I'd like to protose a post...' I was 17 and very nervous. My advice...Practice!"

ოა ჶა ოა

David A Rich, nationally recognized speaker, leading expert on persuasion and rapport, and author of *How to Stay Motivated on a Daily Basis!*, says, "My favorite toast is from the Old Testament of the Bible:

> *May the Lord bless you and keep you;*
> *May the Lord make his face shine upon you and be*
> *gracious to you;*
> *May the Lord lift up his countenance upon you and give*
> *you peace.*

My advise to toasters is to be authentic. Be yourself. A toast can get so vanilla it loses meaning. A toast should reflect the genuine thoughts of the toaster.

∞ ફ∞

Mary Beth Roach, professional speaker, who expertly inpersonates Mae West in many of her speeches:

> *Here's to the kind of room I like—wall to wall men!*
> —Mae West, when admitted to the exclusively male
> Friar's Club in Hollywood

"Check with the people you are toasting beforehand, to see if there is anything they would not like you to say—this way you're sure to avoid tense, embarrassing situations. Also, make sure you are on target for the appropriateness of the toast for the occasion."

∞ ફ∞

Lee Robert, author of *Gendersell™: Selling to the Opposite Sex* and *Cavett Robert: Leaving a Lasting Legacy,* offers this:

Cavett Robert Toast

May the hinges of friendship never rust,
May the wings of love never tear loose a feather,
And may this sacred circle of love grow deeper and
stronger every year,
And not be broken as long as we live.
'Cause they tell me that a bell is not a bell until we ring it,
A song is not a song until we sing it,
Love was not put in our hearts to stay,
Love is only love when we give it away.
So here's to those we love,
And here's to those who love us,
And here's to those that we love
Who love those who love us.
So lets keep this circle of friends and never forget
That life is our greatest gift,
And living nobly, our finest art.
And what we can do, we ought'a do,
And what we ought'a do, we can do;
And what we can do, and ought'a do, I know we will do.
Good luck, God bless, I love everyone of you.

—Cavett Robert, Founder, National Speakers Association (Given with permission by Lee E. Robert, from *Cavett Robert: Leaving a Lasting Legacy,* 1998).

ﱞ ﱞ ﱞ

Dick Semaan, "Stand-up Speaker and Pop-up Toaster," is recipient of NSA's Council of Peer Award of Excellence and presenter of "You're Not getting Older, You're Getting Better," sponsored by Life Care Centers of America. He shares this toast.

Here's to (person's name)... I wish you the best that life has to offer, the simple pleasures which can only be described in the one-syllable words: Love, Joy, Peace, Hope, Faith, Strength, Health, Zeal, and Life! May you experience the fullness of every day with passion, vision, and commitment. May you be better today than you were yesterday, but not as good as you'll be tomorrow.

"Always say and do the things that will focus the eyes and ears of the guests upon the one(s) being toasted. The toast is for the toastee, not the toaster."

∾ ॐ ∾

Somers White, management consultant and professional speaker who has worked in 50 states and six continents, currently residing in Phoenix, contributes this toast—short but compelling.

Here's to the "good old days"—which are now!

"We look back on those wonderful days of the past. Many times we do not stop to realize these are the good old days of later times, but we are experiencing them now."

∾ ॐ ∾

Jeff Slutsky, author of *Streetfighting: Low-Cost Marketing* and *Out-Think, Don't Out-Spend the Competition*, recollects:

"At the reception, after a brief fanfare played, the announcer bellowed, "Ladies and gentlemen, may I present for the first time, Mr. and Mrs. LeBoeuf!" Everyone stood up and applauded as Michael and Elke entered the room and took their seats at the head table. Next, [I] gave this toast:

> *Perhaps one of the most exciting duties of the best man is to give the first toast. I know that Michael in particular was very excited when entering the room today because, in 20 years of professional speaking, this was his first standing ovation. You know, last night at the "awards banquet," Michael told us just how much he and Elke appreciated all of you being with them on this day. In fact, he said that your attendance here was the best gift you could have given him. I just wish he had told me that four weeks ago, before I dropped 300 bucks on a piece of crystal. But be that as it may, everyone now, please lift your glass and join me in wishing Michael and Elke a long and happy life together.*

"A *toast* is a pledge of good intentions, a wish for good health and good things to come to someone or some couple or group. 'Eloquence' is thought on fire," so said the late Ken McFarland, who is considered one of the premier speakers of the first half of the twentieth century. We have to have eloquence in our toasts, and they must have a touch of class about them. A toast should seize the moment. It should offer the audience a hallmark for the occasion, something to take away and remember. It can come as a clever story about the person or some humor that makes a point.

"**Keep it clean.** Off-color material is inappropriate for this type of occasion. After all, you are there to elevate the subjects to a higher level. Why pull the occasion down with poor taste?

"**Beware of alcohol.** The very nature of many occasions introduces alcohol as part of the festivities. If you are speaking, avoid the booze. It thickens the tongue and will cause you and your subjects embarrassment. Most of us have a tough enough time speaking when we are stone sober. To throw booze into the mix makes the occasion impossible.

"**Suit the toast to the occasion.** These are usually happy events. The exceptions are those retirement parties where someone has been forced out of a company. Be sensitive to these *second-tier* issues so that the event does not become a bashing of the company or the subject of the roast.

"**Master's tips for a good toast or roast:** Below are some helpful hints in preparing for your toast or roast:

1. Know the time restraints going in, and suit your comments to the time provided.
2. Try to personalize your comments.
3. Quotes are excellent tools to make your points.
4. There is always room for humor at these occasions, as long as it is appropriate and relative.
5. Humility is the order of the day. After all, the toast is a pledge of good intentions and best wishes for those being toasted.
6. Sincerity is the most important singular attribute of your toast. Believe in what you are sharing."

—From *The Toastmasters International Guide to Successful Speaking*, by Jeff Slutsky and Michael Aun (Dearborn)

Jim Tunney, Ed.D., is "The Dean of NFL Referees," former President of NSA, and author of *Impartial Judgment*. He observes,

> *"Because of my association with pro sports, I am*
> *frequently called upon to 'say a few words' before a*
> *contest or challenge—either sports competitions, or*
> *missions launched by a corporation, organization, or*
> *community group. It is gratifying how often the*
> *following poem (by the world's most prolific writer,*
> *Anonymous) strikes the right chord. The toast, also a*
> *prayer, compels our energy toward honor and dignity—*
> *always a good direction to take.*

"Prayer of a Sportsman"

Dear Lord,
In the battle that goes on through life,
I ask only for a field that is fair,
A chance that is equal to all the strife,
The courage to strive and to dare.
If I should win, let it be by the code,
With my faith and my honor held high;
But if I should lose,
Let me stand by the road,
And cheer as the winners go by.

"The number-one, never-to-be-ignored rule is to *fit the toast to the event*. Be alert to people's sensitivities. Familiarity, gender, age, religion, politics—all such contextual elements deserve respect. The toast-giver who dares not respect them risks throwing egg on his or her face. Remember as well, *a toast is a tribute, not a roast,* and a s*hort* tribute at that. It is not a eulogy, homily, or speech."

∾ ᨋ ∾

Al Walker, "A Big Man with a Big Message," past NSA president, humorous motivational and inspirational keynote speaker:

"All of my toasts fall into one of two categories: They're either real rough and should only be used at bachelor parties—after everyone is solidly inebriated, or they are words from my heart that express the way I feel at that specific moment.

"Don't be silly; you can be funny, and probably should, but there's a difference between silly and funny. Silly usually either draws attention to you or puts down one of the honorees. Funny is usually self-deprecating or pokes positive fun at the honorees."

∾ ⚘ ∾

Mikki Williams is an internationally recognized speaker, consultant, author, trainer, entrepreneur extraordinaire, and mensch. Known for her flamboyant style and infectious energy, she is an inspirational humorist and business motivator.

"My theory is that speaker resources are everywhere, including bathroom stalls in Germany, when I was there delivering speeches. I have learned over the years to keep my eyes and ears open to the messages and information of the universe. I believe many speakers overlook these unusual opportunities. Since I do a lot of consulting with speakers of all levels, I find most people to be very traditional in terms of research and resources. Being known as the consummate rule-breaker, heretic, nonconformist (you get the picture), I am thrilled to find little pearls of wisdom in as many out-of-the-way places as the unexpected allow. As a result, I am always aware of my surroundings, and have found as many "jewels" in unconventional locales as my peers have found rummaging through library books and online reports. Often imitated, but never duplicated.

"In my opinion, toasts can easily be corny or overly sappy, and laughter is always the great equalizer and human bonding agent. That would be my advice to the toasters and toastettes."

∾ ۇ ∾

Dave Yoho, CEO of Dave Yoho Associates, dean of modern sales training and motivation, and author of *How to Have a Good Year Everyday* (Berkeley Press), shares the following toast he uses for individuals he knows well.

You are a unique and precious being created by God for very special purposes. You are ever doing the best you can. You are ever growing in love and awareness. This day is yours. No one can take it away from you.

Here's another favorite:

Peace is not a season.
It is a way of life.
May it be yours.
If you search for the person
You would like to be,
You may never get to enjoy
the person you are.
Peace.
—From *How to Have a Good Year Everyday*©

∾ ۇ ∾

CHAPTER 2

WEDDING TOASTS

If you are asked to give a toast at a wedding, keep in mind that most couples who have weddings of any significant size typically preserve the memories of their special day on video. If for no other reason, avoid drinking heavily before delivering your wedding toast or you can be sure you will never live it down. Wedding toasts can be humorous if you avoid being too personal. Remember, it is likely there are guests in attendance who no one under 70 can even identify.

According to Winifred Gray, in her book, *You and Your Wedding*, proper wedding toast etiquette is as follows:

The father of the bride proposes the first toast to his daughter and his future son-in-law at the engagement party.

The host or father of the groom proposes the first toast to the bride and groom at the rehearsal party.

The best man proposes the first toast to the bride and groom at the wedding reception.

If the bride and groom are seated when toasts are proposed to them, they remain seated, even when others stand. After guests have responded to the toast, the bride and groom drink their wine.

∽ ✿ ∽

May your hearts beat as one from this day forward.

∾ ❦ ∾

On a cold winter's day, two porcupines huddled together to stay warm. Feeling one another's quills, they moved apart. Every time the need for warmth brought them together, their quills would drive them apart. They were driven back and forth at the mercy of their discomforts, until they found the distance from each other that provided both a maximum of comfort and a minimum of pain. May your need for warmth be satisfied, and you be spared the stab of your lover's quills.

∾ ❦ ∾

Here's to the bride and groom, a case of love pure and simple: (Bride) is pure and (Groom) is simple.

∾ ❦ ∾

To (Groom), luckiest man on earth, and to (Bride), the woman who made him that way.

∾ ❦ ∾

Here's to marriage, for man is not complete until he is married...and then he's finished!

∾ ॐ ∾

To your wedding: May your love for each other grow as surely as your waistlines will.

∾ ॐ ∾

Here's to King Solomon, ruler and sage,
The wisest of men in history's age.
He had wives by the thousand, and thought it was fun...
Here's hoping you'll know how to handle just one.

∾ ॐ ∾

May your life be long and sunny, and your husband fat and funny.

∾ ॐ ∾

Here's to the land we love and the love we land.

∾ ⸙ ∾

For a second marriage: "Here's to the triumph of hope over experience."

∾ ⸙ ∾

A toast to love, laughter, and happily ever after.

∾ ⸙ ∾

A toast to the groom— and discretion to his bachelor friends.

∾ ⸙ ∾

Grow old with me!
The best is yet to be,
The last of life
For which the first was made.

∾ ⸙ ∾

Here's to the bride and groom!
May you have a happy honeymoon,
May you lead a happy life,
May you have a bunch of money soon,
And live without all strife.

ও ৯৯ ও

Here's to the husband, and here's to the wife:
May they be lovers for life.

ও ৯৯ ও

Marriage is a wonderful institution—but who wants to
live in an institution?

ও ৯৯ ও

May your joys be as deep as the ocean, and your
misfortunes as light as foam.

ও ৯৯ ও

May your joys be as bright as morning, and your sorrows but shadows that fade in the sunlight of love.

∾ ୫ ∾

May we all live to be present at their Golden Wedding anniversary.

∾ ୫ ∾

May you grow old on one pillow.

∾ ୫ ∾

May you live forever, may I never die.

∾ ୫ ∾

May your love be as endless as your wedding rings.

∾ ୫ ∾

May your wedding days be few, and your anniversaries many.

ം ‌ം

May your future be filled with wine and roses.

ം ‌ം

May your arguments be as long-lived as my New Year's resolutions.

ം ‌ം

To Fate that brought you together, and Love that will keep you happy forever.

ം ‌ം

May the joy you feel today be a pale shadow of that which is to come.

∞ ⧛ ∞

Nothing is nobler or more admirable
Than when two people who see eye to eye live together as husband and wife,
Thereby confounding their enemies and delighting their friends.
—Homer, from The Odyssey

∞ ⧛ ∞

May the rest of your lives be like a bed of roses...without the thorns.

∞ ⧛ ∞

May all your ups and downs be between the sheets.

❧ ❦ ❧

May your love be modern enough to survive the times, and old-fashioned enough to last forever.

❧ ❦ ❧

Here's the husband, here's the wife: May they remain lovers for life.

❧ ❦ ❧

Although outside it is cold and wintry, inside (Bride) and (Groom's) hearts it is warm, and today the seeds of love have been planted. As the spring flowers are soon to bloom, may your love flourish for a sunny season that never ends.

❧ ❦ ❧

May you live together happy and free as the rolling waves on the deep, blue sea.

∿ ❧ ∿

Today, from you and from me, we have made us. What you now do, and what I now do, we do for us. Although you are still you, and I am still me, it is us that is the guide along life's journey and beyond. We do for us, our every thought is for us, now and for always.

∿ ❧ ∿

As two become one—love is eternal.

∿ ❧ ∿

May you never lie, cheat, or drink.
But if you must lie, lie in each other's arms.
And if you must cheat, cheat death.
But if you must drink, drink with all of us because we love you.

∿ ❧ ∿

Marriage is a lot like the army; everyone complains, but you'd be surprised at the large number that re-enlist.

∽ ❦ ∽

(Bride), please put your hand on the table. Now (Groom), put your hand on top of (Bride's) hand. I want everyone in the room to see the last time that (Groom) has the upper hand!

∽ ❦ ∽

May you share a joy that grows deeper, a friendship that grows closer, and a marriage that grows richer through the years.

∽ ❦ ∽

May the road you now travel together be filled with much love and success.

∽ ❦ ∽

May you share equally in each others' love, and may all your troubles be little ones.

∾ ﴾ ∾

May your hands be forever clasped in friendship and your hearts forever joined in love.

∾ ﴾ ∾

Let us live for the future and learn from the past; because the knowledge you gain will make your marriage last.

∾ ﴾ ∾

Perchance to dream, perchance is right! You won't get a chance to dream tonight.

∾ ﴾ ∾

May your good times be plenty, your sad times be few;
May your love grow brighter with each day, and with
each day begin anew.

∾ ૐ ∾

As you set out to write a new chapter in your life as
husband and wife, may your union be like a game of
poker: start as a pair and end with a full house.

∾ ૐ ∾

A wedding wish: May you never forget what is worth
remembering, or remember what is worth forgetting.

∾ ૐ ∾

I would like to thank the parents of the bride and
groom, for without them, this day would not be possible.

∾ ૐ ∾

Here's to the bride and mothers-in-law;
Here's to the groom and fathers-in-law;
Here's to the sisters and brothers-in-law;
Here's to the brothers and sisters-in-law;
Here's to good friends and friends-in-law;
May none of them need an attorney-at-law!

∾ ૹ ∾

We wish them the best of luck, but know that they don't
need it, because they have the best of love.

∾ ૹ ∾

May your love build for you an indestructible
community of two, and may your married life be as
loving as it is long. To the bride and groom!

∾ ૹ ∾

Roses are red, violets are fine, hope your marriage is as
happy as mine.

∾ ૹ ∾

Let us toast the health of the Bride,
Let us toast the health of the Groom.
Let us toast the person that tied,
Let us toast every guest in the room.

❧ ❦ ❧

Look down you gods
And on this couple drop a blessed crown.
—William Shakespeare

❧ ❦ ❧

A commitment should last forever, and life should
always be this good. But when times are hard and the
road is rough, remember the words you spoke today,
remember the way you feel right now, and try to forgive.
Sometimes that's all we have to give. For to love is to
learn, and to learn is to forgive. Best wishes to you both,
and may your love be long-lived.

❧ ❦ ❧

May all your children have wealthy parents!

❧ ❦ ❧

I wish both of you the patience of Job, the wisdom of
Solomon, and the children of Israel.

ᔆ ᔖ ᔆ

To our beautiful bride:
May she always stay happy and nice,
With all the love in her eyes,
Not to mention being so witty and wise;
Of that no one can deny,
Specially by the groom, that's why.

And to our handsome groom:
May he stay as romantic and true;
A husband, the role he'll assume,
Tell him, for he has no clue;
Everyday a flower or some perfume,
To make her smile and never be blue.

ᔆ ᔖ ᔆ

Health to you, wealth to you,
The best that life can give to you.
Happiness be true to you,
And life be long and good to you.

ᔆ ᔖ ᔆ

And here's to the groom with the bride so fair,
And here's to the bride with the groom so rare,
May everyday be happier than the last!

❧

Welcome to the next chapter in your life! May your book
of life have a happy ending.

❧

Never above you,
Never below you,
Always beside you.

❧

With a past like ours, who needs a future? Well my
friend, yours is sitting beside you!

❧

May you always be each other's best friend,
May your honeymoon be filled with smiles and
laughter,
And may you live happily married ever after.

❧

Don't look for the perfect spouse in each other, try to be
the perfect spouse for each other.

❧

May your marriage be like fine wine, getting better and
better with age.

❧

Here's to (Bride and Groom):
May your years together be as wonderful as today,
May your sorrows be few and your joys be countless.
And may a flight of angels carry you as one from this
day forward.

❧

May you both have the patience to listen.

❧ ✿ ❧

May the sparkle in your eyes light your path for the years to come.

❧ ✿ ❧

To the groom: The great philosopher Confucius once said, "Bigamy means having one wife too many." Some say monogamy means the same thing.

❧ ✿ ❧

May your obstetrician find your babies so beautiful that he delivers them free!

❧ ✿ ❧

A favorite at cannibal weddings: "May the skin of your bum never cover a drum."

꙰ ꙮ ꙰

May you live long lives, doing what you love together. And when the time comes for you to pass away, may you die as you lived, doing what you love together.

꙰ ꙮ ꙰

May you love each other more than yesterday, but less than tomorrow.

꙰ ꙮ ꙰

May you be poor in misfortune and rich in blessings. May you be slow to make enemies and quick to make friends. But rich or poor, quick or slow, may you know nothing but happiness from this day forward.

꙰ ꙮ ꙰

I would wish you good luck, but I never wish luck on a sure thing.

∾ ❧ ∾

Standing next to each other, facing the world, and you always able to say, "This is my beloved, this is my friend."

∾ ❧ ∾

They say that marriage is an institution. And I can't think of two people who should be institutionalized more than this bride and groom.

∾ ❧ ∾

May the twinkle in your eyes stay with you, and the love in your hearts never fade.

∾ ❧ ∾

...And remember, on any disagreement the husband is entitled to the last few words. And those words are, "Yes, dear."

∾ ફ∾ ∾

Down the hatch to a striking match!

∾ ફ∾ ∾

*May you always be lovers, but most of all friends,
And share with each other whatever life sends.*

∾ ફ∾ ∾

*May your lifetime together be full and complete,
And your kisses together be deep, warm, and sweet.*

∾ ફ∾ ∾

(Bride) and (Groom) are like epoxy: Separate they are perpetually sticky, like sap. But together they form a rock-hard bond.

ഇ ‍ൠ ഇ

Now you will feel no rain, for each of you will be shelter to the other. Now you will feel no cold, for each of you will be warmth to the other. Now there is no more loneliness. Now there are two persons, but one life before you. Go now to your dwelling, to enter in to the days of your life together. And may your days be good and long upon the Earth.
—From an Apache Indian Wedding Ceremony

ഇ ‍ൠ ഇ

May the love you share forever remain as beautiful as the bride looks today.

ഇ ‍ൠ ഇ

Toasts for All Occasions

To keep a marriage brimming,
With love in the loving cup,
Whenever you're wrong, admit it,
Whenever you're right, shut-up!

ॐ ॐ ॐ

May your joys exceed sorrows, may your ecstasy exceed
pain, may your unselfish love exceed your selfishness,
may you live for the sake of each other, and may the
bounty of this life be in abundance!

ॐ ॐ ॐ

May all your days be filled with sunshine, all your
nights with romance, and all the time in between with
love. The love of your parents has brought you this far;
now may your love for each other carry you forward this
day and always.

ॐ ॐ ॐ

Here's a toast to the lovely bride,
And to the husband by her side.
Here's a toast to the home they are going to share,
May love and trust dwell with them there.
Here's to the husband, here's to the wife.
May they remain lovers all of their life.

∽ ॐ ∽

May your joys exceed sorrows, may your ecstacy exceed
pain, and your unselfish love exceed your selfishness,
may you live for the sake of the other, and may the
bounty of this life be in abundance!

∽ ॐ ∽

Chapter 3

Anniversary Toasts

When giving an anniversary toast, the couple receiving the honor should be afforded the same joy and illusion of romantic possiblities no matter what the circumstances of the lives together might be. In other words, if you are throwing a 40th wedding anniversary party for your parents and, although you love them, you know they more closely resemble the World Federation Wrestlers than Ozzie and Harriet, it's not the time nor place to behave like your inner child. Anniversary toasts can be amusing but should never be insulting. The best loved anniversary toasts are those that bring the couple back to the time they said their "I do's." If the couple is particularly romantic, you can adapt any of the wedding toasts to fit the occasion.

∞ ❧ ∞

Here's to loving, to romance, to us:
May we travel together through time.
We alone count as none, but together we're one.
For our partnership puts love to rhyme.

∞ ❧ ∞

Here's to you both,
A beautiful pair,
On the birthday of
Your love affair.

∾ 🦢 ∾

Let anniversaries come, and anniversaries go—but may
your happiness continue forever.

∾ 🦢 ∾

Here's a toast to the many good times you've enjoyed
together...and to the one or two that you just tolerated.

∾ 🦢 ∾

May the warmth of your affections survive the frosts of age.

∼ ❧ ∼

To your coming anniversaries—may they be outnumbered by your coming pleasures.

∼ ❧ ∼

Here's to the man who loves his wife,
And loves his wife alone.
For many a man loves another man's wife,
When he ought to be loving his own.

∼ ❧ ∼

Here's to you who halves my sorrows and doubles my joys.

∾ ≬ ∾

I have known many,
Liked a few,
Loved one—
Here's to you!

∾ ≬ ∾

Let us drink to love, which is nothing unless it is divided by two.

∾ ≬ ∾

Love doesn't make the world go around; love is what makes the ride worthwhile.

ɔ ʃ ɔ

A toast to your anniversary: You've had many good years together, either that or one helluva prenuptial agreement.

ɔ ʃ ɔ

The love you give away is the only love you keep.

ɔ ʃ ɔ

May your love be as endless as your wedding rings.

ɔ ʃ ɔ

Toasts for All Occasions

New love is silver,
Wait for the rest;
Old love is gold love,
Old love is best.

ఌ ૐ ఌ

A toast to your anniversary and the love that has held you together these many years: When times are good, it's easy, brother. When times are tough is when you need one another.

ఌ ૐ ఌ

To marriage: An exercise that works every muscle in the human spirit.

ఌ ૐ ఌ

May you always look into each other's eyes as you did the night you first met.

∾ ❧ ∾

May you have the best life has to offer.

∾ ❧ ∾

Love each other as you would your children: unconditionally!

∾ ❧ ∾

May the twinkle in your eyes stay with you, and the love in your hearts never fade.

∾ ❧ ∾

Joy to you on your anniversary. From this day forward may you be blessed with the same happiness your union has brought to those around you.

∾ ❧ ∾

May you be blessed with happiness and love that deepens every year.

∾ ❧ ∾

May you celebrate a very happy anniversary with tender moments, love, and cherished memories.

∾ ❧ ∾

To my beloved on our anniversary. I love you more with every passing year.

∽ ❦ ∽

May your love be reflected in the souls of your children.

∽ ❦ ∽

To my twin soul. As the years pass we become more and more as one.

∽ ❦ ∽

CHAPTER 4

BIRTHDAY
TOASTS

Birthdays are great opportunities for toasts of all kinds. When young people have significant birthdays such as 16 or 21, it is perfectly acceptable to make them the subject of reasonable jokes or roasts. But keep in mind that if the birthday boy or girl is over 30, you may be stomping on sacred territory. Not everyone has a thick skin about certain aspects of aging.

For example, toasts referring to anything sagging are to be reserved for only the closest of friends. Even then they can be risky. Birthdays are also an opportunity to be sentimental. Although some people protest, we are all big kids at heart and enjoy being the center of attention for that one special day. Sometimes the greatest gift you can give to a person is a statement sent from your heart.

∾ ⧫ ∾

To a healthy year, and many of them.

∾ ⧫ ∾

Birthdays were never like this when I had them.
Although another year has passed,
She's no older than the last!

∾ 🕮 ∾

May everything about your day be just the way you
want. Have a happy and wonderful birthday and life.

∾ 🕮 ∾

Another candle on your cake?
Well, that's no cause to pout.
Be glad that you have strength enough
To blow the darn thing out!

∾ 🕮 ∾

There are some people who pass through your life like a butterfly. They rarely make contact and then are quickly gone. There are those who pass through your life like fellow travelers. They sit and talk for awhile on the airplane, but upon touchdown, they drift away toward their own destinations. Then there are people who pass through your life and decide to set up camp. They work with you, share with you, borrow from you, care about you. These are the kind that give meaning to life.
(Name) falls into that latter category. To my dear friend, I wish a happy birthday and an exciting rest of her life.

ტ ჶ ტ

Happy Birthday to you,
And many to be,
With friends that are true
As you are to me.

ტ ჶ ტ

Another year older? Think this way: Just one day older than yesterday.

ტ ჶ ტ

Someone has said that a friend is someone who understands your past, believes in your future, and accepts you today just the way you are. (Name) has been just that kind of person. That's why his birthday is as special to me as my very own. Happy birthday to a very special person.

ལ ࣷ ལ

Do not resist growing old; many are denied the privilege.

ལ ࣷ ལ

Here's to you! No matter how old you are, you don't look it!

ལ ࣷ ལ

Birthdays are a time to celebrate—the memories of days gone by, the joys of the moment, and the dreams of tomorrow. We're celebrating with you.

May you live to be a hundred years, with one extra year to repent.

You're only as old as you are.

To your birthday, glass held high;
Glad it's you that's older, and not I.

There's a time to be born and a time to die, and what happens in the interval in between is of great importance. (Name), of all the people I know, you've made the most of that interval. Just think of this birthday as a green light on the road of your dreams. Happiness to you.

∾ ⚘ ∾

May you live to be 120.

∾ ⚘ ∾

In many ways, (name), You've been like a son/daughter to me—pouty, arrogant, disrespectful. Seriously, I'd be awfully proud to have a son/daughter just like you. Here's to a happy, happy birthday.

∾ ⚘ ∾

Just remember that when you get over the hill, you pick up speed on the downside. But you have no cause to worry. The faster you go, the better you get. Here's to a great birthday.

∾ ໄ. ∾

To a wonderful (brother, sister) who has always been good enough to be older than me.

∾ ໄ. ∾

From father to son; or mother to daughter:
When you were born I saw in you all of the things I had dreamed for myself
Now I see that you are more than I could have imagined.
Happy birthday (son, daughter). May all of the dreams you have for yourself come true.

∾ ໄ. ∾

Though you see yourself as getting older, we see your birthday as a reminder of how many happy times you have brought into our lives. To many more birthdays that we can share with you.

ལ ཧ ལ

Thank you (dad, mom) for always being there for me. On this, your special day, may you be wined and dined like royalty but remember to give the bill to my (brother, sister.)

ལ ཧ ལ

To a (brother, sister) who I am honored to call my friend.

ལ ཧ ལ

To a friend who has taught me what it must be like to have a (brother, sister.)

๏ ๏ ๏

For a significant birthday representing a change in a person's status (for example, 10, 13, 16, 18, 21) you can say the following:
As you reach this new chapter in your life, may you discover that it is you who will write your own story and may you always have a pencil on hand.

๏ ๏ ๏

You are now a (man, woman.) May you be blessed with the confidence that you can learn from your mistakes.

๏ ๏ ๏

Chapter 5

Toasts
For Friends

Giving a toast on behalf of a friend can be fun and it can be rewarding. It is so easy to take friendship for granted. When you have an occasion to raise a glass or bottle or keg of something in good cheer, to someone you care about, even the least touchy-feely among us can let fly with some sentiment. Buddies and girlfriends are an important part of life. Aside from gender-bashing toasts reserved for girls' and guys' night out, there may be times when you want to say something meaningful.

∽ ❧ ∽

Here's a toast to the future,
A sigh for the past;
We can love and remember,
And hope to the last.
And for all the base lies
That the almanacs hold,
While there's love in the heart,
We can never grow old.

∽ ❧ ∽

May fortune still be kind to you,
And happiness be true to you,
And life be long and good to you,
Is the toast of all our friends to you.

ᙯ ᖟᕊ ᙯ

Friendship: May differences of opinion cement it.

ᙯ ᖟᕊ ᙯ

Here's to cold nights, warm friends, and a good drink to give them.

ᙯ ᖟᕊ ᙯ

May our house always be too small to hold all our friends.

∼ 🍷 ∼

Here's to our friends, and the strength to put up with them.

∼ 🍷 ∼

Friendship is the wine of life: Let's drink of it and to it.

∼ 🍷 ∼

However rare true love is, true friendship is rarer.

∼ 🍷 ∼

Don't walk in front of me,
I may not follow.
Don't walk behind me,
I may not lead.
Walk beside me,
And just be my friend.

∾ ₷ ∾

Here's to a friend: He knows you well and likes you just
the same.

∾ ₷ ∾

Here's to friendship,
May it be reckoned,
Long as a lifetime,
Close as a second.

∾ ₷ ∾

May the friends of our youth be the companions of our old age.

∾ ફ∾ ∾

The Lord gives us our relatives—thank God we can choose our friends.

∾ ફ∾ ∾

Here's to tall ships, here's to small ships, here's to all the ships in the sea. But the best ships are friendships: Here's to you and me!

∾ ફ∾ ∾

Toasts for All Occasions

May the hinges of friendship never rust, nor the wings of love lose a feather.

∾ ₽ ∾

May we have more and more friends, and need them less and less.

∾ ₽ ∾

Here's to you, old friend,
May you live a thousand years,
Just to sort of cheer things up,
This vale of human tears.
And may I live a thousand too—
A thousand, less one day,
'Cause I wouldn't care to be on earth,
And hear you'd passed away.

∾ ₽ ∾

To our best friends, who know the worst about us, but refuse to believe it.

❧ ⚘ ❧

Old friends are scarce,
New friends are few,
Here's hoping I find,
One of each in you.

❧ ⚘ ❧

May you have the strength to change those things that can be changed,
May you have the patience to live with those things that cannot be changed,
May you have the wisdom to know one from the other!

❧ ⚘ ❧

May good fortune precede you, may love walk with you, may good friends follow you.

❧ ⚘ ❧

CHAPTER 6

RETIREMENT TOASTS

When giving a business or retirement toast, the most important thing to keep in mind is that in any business setting there is an invisible line between business and personal. As much as our work environments have become secondary or even primary homes to us, it is best not to let your guard down too much. There is the old expression, "Thou shalt not dip thy pen in company ink." Which can also be described in another way that shall be referred to here only through innuendo, it has to do with not performing bodily functions in the same place in which you take your meals. You get the point. So have fun toasting your boss for having a doubled bottom line, just don't make fun of his or her spouse. Retirement parties can be fun, but remember, you will be returning to work on Monday.

>-+-+>-0-<+-+-<

Here's to doing nothing at all
Relax, enjoy, and just have a ball.
When you're sitting at home with nothing to do,
Think of us still at work. We're doing that too.

>-+-+>-0-<+-+-<

When you have finished your work and the day is done,
It's time to kick up your heels and have some fun.

><

To a (man, woman) who has contributed greatly to the
success of this business. We know that whatever you do
you will touch the lives of those around you.

><

As you negotiate the days of your life, may you always
keep your leverage.

><

Here's to Florida winters. (Substitute appropriate
venues.)

><

Remember when you have nothing to do,
That no one does that better than you.

><+@>-o-<+><

Gardening, reading, golf, and fishing,
May you lead the life for which we have all been
wishing.

><+@>-o-<+><

To you: You did it...whatever it is.

><+@>-o-<+><

Good-bye to you. As you walk this new road of life
remember those you've left behind.

><+@>-o-<+><

To our company visionary who delivers the profits.

><+@>-o-<+><

May your retirement bring you all the joy you have been wishing for and may you know happiness all the days of your life.

⊱────◦────⊰

May all that you have contributed to this company pay off in fish and birdies.

⊱────◦────⊰

To our most valuable player. You've helped us have a winning team.

⊱────◦────⊰

To our best idea man/woman, who sees beyond the bottom line.

⊱────◦────⊰

CHAPTER 7

TOASTS FOR "GIRLS' NIGHT OUT" AND "GUYS' NIGHT OUT"

The best thing about "girls' night" or "guys' night out" toasts is that they are never intended for the ears of the opposite sex. So be outrageous, and enjoy having an audience of close friends. Friends of the same gender have can have fun letting off steam about the things they will never comprehend about the opposite sex.

Here are some ideas to get you started. But surely do not limit yourself to these. Just make sure you have at least one designated driver.

"Girls' Night Out"

Here's to you, here's to me,
In hopes we never disagree.
But if we do, the hell with you...
Here's to me!

∾ ⚜ ∾

Toasts for All Occasions

Here's to the woman who is thrifty,
And knows it's folly to yearn,
And picks out a lover of 50
Because he has money to burn.

∽ ❀ ∽

May we kiss those we please, and please those we kiss.

∽ ❀ ∽

I'll drink to the gentleman I think is most entitled to it;
for if anyone can drive me to drink, he can certainly do
it.

∽ ❀ ∽

Here's to husbands and sweethearts. May they never meet!

∾ ᏭᎭ ∾

Men are somewhat like sausage,
Very smooth upon the skin;
But you can never tell exactly
How much hog there is within.

∾ ᏭᎭ ∾

To man: The only animal that laughs, drinks when he is not thirsty, and makes love at all seasons of the year.

∾ ᏭᎭ ∾

To the men I've loved,
To the men I've kissed,
My heartfelt apologies
To the men I've missed.

∾ ❦ ∾

Women's faults are many,
Men have only two...
Everything they say,
And everything they do.

∾ ❦ ∾

Here's to God's first thought: Man!
Here's to God's second thought: Woman!
Second thoughts are always better.

∾ ❦ ∾

Here's to you and here's to me,
And here's to love and laughter.
I'll be true as long as you,
And not a minute after!

∾ ❧ ∾

Here's to the men we love,
And here's to the men that love us.
But the men we love aren't the men who love us,
So screw the men and here's to us!

∾ ❧ ∾

Here's to never breaking plans with friends to go out
with a guy!

∾ ❧ ∾

Here's to power shopping without a credit limit.

∾ ও ∾

"Guys' Night Out"

A piece of cowboy advice: There are two theories to arguing with a woman. Neither one works.

>-+-0-+-<

Here's to good, old whiskey, so amber and so clear: 'Tis not as sweet as a woman's lips, but a damn sight more sincere.

>-+-0-+-<

Here's to my mother-in-law, who still calls me a son—but I never let her finish the sentence.

>-+-0-+-<

Here's to the woman of my dreams, who looks like a million bucks...and is just as hard to make.

Here's to love, a love that will linger. I gave her the ring... and she gave me the finger.

Here's to the man who takes a wife:
Let him make no mistake.
For it makes a lot of difference
Whose wife you take.

Here's to passing gas loudly, in bed or any place that I like.

Here's to eating pizza for breakfast, lunch, and dinner.

CHAPTER 8

ROMANTIC TOASTS

Candlelight, soft music, good food, and an expectant glance from your spouse, date, or lover. You raise your glass and pause. Your mouth goes dry and you can hear your heart pound. Is it love? No, it is the fear that whatever comes out of your mouth had better be good. Whether you are the man or woman in charge of delivering the romantic toast, you know it can have a great impact on the course of the evening or even the course of your lives together. Romantic toasts should be delivered from the heart with a great deal of eye contact. If the truth be known, when two hearts are open to one another, whatever is said will be perfect. However, these toasts may help you for those moments when you want to be sure to be prepared.

∾ ໃ∾ ∾

To the one I love: May our lives together be blessed with happiness and peace.

∾ ໃ∾ ∾

To us.

~ ❦ ~

To your beautiful eyes; they are windows to a beautiful soul.

~ ❦ ~

May our love be as strong as the willow, and as willing to bend.

~ ❦ ~

If you are ever afraid, or feeling alone, remember this night and how much I love you.

~ ❦ ~

I have never wanted to be so close to another human being that I would care more about them than I do about myself. May we hold this moment forever. To us.

∾ ૢ૾ ∾

To the (blue, brown) of your eyes and the green in your wallet. Just kidding. To the (blue, brown) of your eyes and all the credit we need.

∾ ૢ૾ ∾

To a wonderful man/woman, who is both a friend and a lover.

∾ ૢ૾ ∾

Your eyes are like a country sky in the autumn. When I am with you I feel free to be myself. Here's to my best friend and only love.

∾ ⧉ ∾

To the (woman, man) who shares the good times and bad. Here's to the good times.

∾ ⧉ ∾

When God created souls and sent them into the world, he knew all along that someday ours would find each other. To my eternal soulmate.

∾ ⧉ ∾

To our success. Without you, it would all be meaningless.

∾ ᥫ᭡ ∾

You have given me a home in your arms. Since I met you, I have learned what it is to be loved. God bless our lives together.

∾ ᥫ᭡ ∾

To our life together. As we walk the path of life, always know my hand is within your reach.

∾ ᥫ᭡ ∾

May we always remember the blessings of love.

❧ ❦ ❧

You are my rose and my candlelight. Wherever you are there is love.

❧ ❦ ❧

To the most beautiful person in the world. Thank you for sharing my life.

❧ ❦ ❧

The sun sets and rises in your eyes. To us.

ॐ ॐ ॐ

You have been so supportive of my search for myself.
What I have discovered along the way is that I love you.
To you—and now—to us.

ॐ ॐ ॐ

To you, my inspiration, my light, my love.

ॐ ॐ ॐ

May you never know the pain of uncertainty. You can
always count on my love.

ॐ ॐ ॐ

To all the memories we have shared and the new ones we are creating.

❧ ❦ ❧

With you I believe I can do anything. To us and a life full of prosperity.

❧ ❦ ❧

There are so many things I wish I could say to describe how I feel about you. Please trust that in these simple words are a lifetime of dreams. To us.

❧ ❦ ❧

CHAPTER 9

SPIRITUAL TOASTS

There are many occasions that lend themselves to religious or spiritual toasts. The important thing to remember is that you may have a mixture of many traditions at any one event.

If you know that the toastee has strong preferences for a particular path you can have more leeway in choosing a toast that is more direct. For example, you can use Jesus in a toast if you know the toastee is a devout Christian. It is not appropriate for you to use a toast with the name of Jesus if *you* are a devout Christian but the toastee is of a different faith. In this time we are a bit more willing to be open about spirituality. There are many toasts that use a more generic sense of spirituality as opposed to defining exactly what that means for any particular group. It is likely that a sincere spiritual toast will not only be well-received but will be uplifting for those sharing in it with you.

➤━◆━◆━O━◆━◆━◀

May the Lord love us, but not call us too soon.

➤━◆━◆━O━◆━◆━◀

Grandchildren are gifts of God.

>—+◆—O—◆+—◄

Children are God's way of compensating us for growing old.

>—+◆—O—◆+—◄

To the Great Unknown—who is waiting to do us a favor.

>—+◆—O—◆+—◄

Eat thy bread with joy, and drink thy wine with a merry heart.
—Ecclesiastes 9:10

>—+◆—O—◆+—◄

Here's to Eternity—may we spend it in as good company as this night finds us.

>++++O++++<

As the two of you now become one through this holy marriage in witness of God, and all friends here, may He bless you with Faith, Hope and Charity; Faith - to believe in God, Hope—to love and support each other, Charity—to remember and love each person that touches your lives.

>++++O++++<

May you love your husband, and you love your wife, like Jesus loves you both.

>++++O++++<

May the Lord, God be over all in your life, and may each of you be first in one another's life so you both will have a joyous and fulfilling lifetime of oneness in our Lord.

>++++O++++<

Father of fathers, make me one,
A fit example for a son.

>-+-#-+-O-+-<#>-+-<

A toast to our bride and groom:
Perfect, total love between a man and woman is like a
flaming ball of fire, composed of four layers.
The outer layer of the ball of love is the flame of passion
for one another. May you possess it all of your lives.
The second layer of the ball is that of liking each other,
with its ebbs and flows. May your ebbs always be less
frequent than your flows.
The third layer is that of friendship. May you always
find your best friend in each other.
The fourth and inner layer is the hard, firm core of
Decision, shown to us perfectly by our Lord. This is the
same love found in the Bible, in Corinthians 13. May
you be constant in your decision to love each other
always. And may you have this perfect, total love
forever.

>-+-#-+-O-+-<#>-+-<

May you be truly happy by loving each other and
agreeing wholeheartedly with each other, working
together with one heart and mind and purpose.
—Adapted from Phillipians 2:2

>-+-#-+-O-+-<#>-+-<

*May the Lord of all creation bless you and become part
of your daily lives. May the perfect, selfless love He
showed all of us be the love you have for each other. May
each of you always seek to be the perfect mate, and in so
doing have the perfect mate. May those of us who love
you, love you as one, as you will become.*

>+·+@·+O·+@·+<

Love each other as God loves you, unconditionally.

To the Bride and Groom:
May you have the courage *to create a life unique to your
vision of the world.*
May you have the tolerance *to allow the other to grow,
according to his or her own path, and at his or her own pace.*
May you understand that self protection *does not mean
mistrust.*
May you each have enough self love *to receive the love each
has to give.*
May you grow beyond the limits of your individual egos *to
fully surrender to love.*
And may you both embrace the Godlove *that forms the center
of your union.*
—Excerpted from "The Seven Lessons©" by
    Deborah Herman, 1998

>+·+@·+O·+@·+<

Here's to the guiding light of our congregation.

May the great spirit guide your walk.

May you find the serenity of oneness.

To a loving soul. May all the goodness you have given to this world be sent back to you tenfold.

May you find the truth you seek, without ever forgetting the question.

May you reap what you sow.

✠

*Never be afraid to trust an unknown future to a
known God.*
—Corrie Ten Boom

✠

*Where there is doubt, faith.
Where there is despair, hope.
Where there is darkness, light.
Where there is sadness, joy.
Oh Divine Master, grant that I might not so much seek
to be consoled as to console.
To be understood as to understand.
To be loved as to love.
It is in giving that we receive.
It is in pardoning that we are pardoned.
And it is in denying that we are born to eternal life.*

✠

CHAPTER 10

IRISH

TOASTS

When you read Irish toasts they make you feel like you can be included in the celebration no matter who you are. They are warm, funny, sincere, and show a love of life overshadowed only by a love of good whiskey. We have included a disproportionate amount of Irish toasts in this book because we were able to find so many that were good. Whether it is St. Patrick's day or any day of the year, you can find a toast from this list that should suit your occasion. Perhaps the best introduction to this section is to quote an Irish toast: "There are only two kinds of people in the world: the Irish and those who wish they were."

><+>+O+<+>+<

Here's to the health of all those that we love,
Here's to the health of all those that love us,
Here's to the health of all those that live them...
That love those,
That love them,
That love those,
That love us.

><+>+O+<+>+<

*May you get all your wishes but one
So you always have something to strive for.*

God speed the plow and bless the cornmow.

*God invented whiskey so the Irish wouldn't rule the
world.*

*It's better to spend money like there's no tomorrow,
than to spend tonight like there's no money.*

*Get on your knees and thank the Lord you're on your
feet.*

May your glasses ever be full.
May the roof over your head be always strong.
And may you be in heaven half an hour
Before the devil knows you're dead.

>-+*-•-0-•*-+-<

Here's to long life and a merry one.
A quick death and an easy one.
A pretty girl and an honest one.
A cold beer—and another one!

>-+*-•-0-•*-+-<

An old Irish recipe for longevity:
Leave the table hungry.
Leave the bed sleepy.
Leave the table thirsty.

>-+*-•-0-•*-+-<

May the enemies of Ireland never meet a friend.

>-+*-•-0-•*-+-<

Always remember to forget
The things that made you sad.
But never forget to remember
The things that made you glad.

Always remember to forget
The friends that proved untrue.
But never forget to remember
Those who have stuck by you.

Always remember to forget
The troubles that passed away.
But never forget to remember
The blessings that come each day.

May the blessings of each day
Be the blessings you need most.

>-+-#-+-O-+-#-+-<

May the joys of today
Be those of tomorrow.
The goblets of life
Hold no dregs of sorrow.

>-+-#-+-O-+-#-+-<

Here's to thee and me and aw' of us!
May we ne'er want naught, none of us!
Neither thee nor me nor anybody else,
Aw on is—nawn of us.

>-+-#-+-O-+-#-+-<

St. Patrick was a gentleman
Who through strategy and stealth
Drove all the snakes from Ireland.
Here's toasting to his health.
But not too many toastings
Lest you lose yourself, and then
Forget the good St. Patrick
And see all those snakes again.

May you have:
No frost on your spuds,
No worms on your cabbage.
May your goat give plenty of milk.
And if you inherit a donkey,
May she be in foal.

May the luck of the Irish possess you.
May the devil fly off with your worries.
May God bless you forever and ever.

Toasts for All Occasions

May the luck of the Irish
Lead to happiest heights
And the highway you travel
Be lined with green lights.

May your heart be warm and happy
With the lilt of Irish laughter
Every day in every way
And forever and ever after.

May the strength of three be in your journey.

May brooks and trees and singing hills
Join in the chorus too.
And every gentle wind that blows
Send happiness to you.

May the face of every good news
And the back of every bad news
Be toward us.

>+++>+O++>+++<

May you have the food and raiment,
A soft pillow for your head,
May you be forty years in heaven
Before the devil knows you're dead.

>+++>+O++>+++<

May your right hand always
Be stretched out in friendship
And never in want.

>+++>+O++>+++<

Here's to a sweetheart, a bottle and a friend.
The first beautiful, the second full, the last ever faithful.

>+++>+O++>+++<

Toasts for All Occasions

May the grass grow long on the road to hell for want of use.

Here's that we may always have
A clean shirt
A clean conscience
And a punt in your pocket.

May I see you gray,
And combing your grandchildren's hair.

Bless you and yours
As well as the cottage you live in.
May the roof overhead be well-thatched
And those inside by well-matched.

May the hand of a friend always be near you,
And may God fill your heart with gladness to cheer you.

>――·●·―○―·●·―<

May those who love us love us,
And those that don't love us,
May God turn their hearts.
And if He doesn't turn their hearts
May he turn their ankles,
So we'll know them by their limping.

>――·●·―○―·●·―<

Merry met, and merry part,
I drink to thee with all my heart.

>――·●·―○―·●·―<

Here's to the fellow who smiles
When life runs along like a song.
And here's to the lad who can smile
When everything goes dead wrong.

>――·●·―○―·●·―<

Toasts for All Occasions

May you live all the days of your life.
—Jonathan Swift, Anglo-Irish writer

⭠•✦•O•✦•⭢

May the Good Lord take a liking to you...but not too soon!

⭠•✦•O•✦•⭢

As you slide down the banister of life,
May the splinters never point the wrong way.

⭠•✦•O•✦•⭢

Here's to temperance supper,
With water glasses tall,
And coffee and tea to end with—
And me not there at all!

⭠•✦•O•✦•⭢

If you're lucky enough to be Irish...
You're lucky enough!

>-+-●-+-○-+-●-+-<

May the leprechauns be near you,
To spread good luck along your way.
And may all the Irish angels,
Smile upon you St. Patrick's Day.

>-+-●-+-○-+-●-+-<

Health and a long life to you.
Land without rent to you.
A child every year to you.
And if you can't go to heaven,
May you at least die in Ireland.

>-+-●-+-○-+-●-+-<

May you live long,
Die happy,
And rate a mansion in heaven.

>-+-●-+-○-+-●-+-<

There are only two kinds of people in the world:
The Irish,
And those who wish they were.

May your troubles be less
And your blessings be more.
And nothing but happiness
Come through your door.

Here's to you and yours
And to mine and ours.
And if mine and ours
Ever come across to you and yours,
I hope you and yours will do
As much for mine and ours
As mine and ours have done
For you and yours!

May the Lord keep you in his hand
And never close His fist too tight.

May your thoughts be as glad as the shamrocks.
May your heart be as light as a song.
May each day bring you bright hours,
That stay with you all year long.
For each petal on the shamrock
This brings a wish your way—
Good health, good luck, and happiness
For today and every day.

Wherever you go and whatever you do,
May the luck of the Irish be there with you.

May the blessings of light be upon you,
Light without and light within.
And in all your comings and goings,
May you ever have a kindly greeting
From them you meet on the road.

May you be poor in misfortune,
Rich in blessings,
Slow to make enemies,
And quick to make friends.
But rich or poor, quick or slow,
May you know nothing but happiness
From this day forward.

>⊱⋅•◦•⋅⊰

Here's to the four hinges of society.
May you fight, steal, lie and drink.
When you fight, may you fight for your country.
When you steal, may you steal away from bad company.
When you lie, may you lie at the side of your sweetheart.
And when you drink, may you drink with me.

>⊱⋅•◦•⋅⊰

A journalist invents his lies, and rams them down
your throat.
So stay at home, and drink your beer, and let the
neighbors vote.
—William Butler Yeats, Irish poet

>⊱⋅•◦•⋅⊰

Like the goodness of the five loaves and two fishes,
Which God divided among the five thousand men,
May the blessing of the King who so divided
Be upon our share of this common meal.

The health of all Ireland,
and the County of Mayo,
And when that much is dead,
May we still be on the go.

May peace and plenty be the first
To lift the latch on your door,
And happiness be guided to your home
By the candle of Christmas.

Forsake not an old friend, for the new is not comparable
to him.
A new friend is a new wine: When it is old, thou shalt
drink it with pleasure.

Toasts for All Occasions

May there be a fox on your fishing hook
And a hare on your bait
And may you kill no fish
Until St. Brigid's Day.

Here's to beefsteak when you're hungry,
Whiskey when you're dry,
All the women you'll ever want,
And heaven when you die.

Who is a friend but someone to toast,
Someone to gibe, someone to roast.
My friends are the best friends
Loyal, willing and able.
Now let's get to drinking!
Glasses off the table!

May you have warm words on a cold evening,
A full moon on a dark night,
And the road downhill all the way to your door.
Here's to your health and prosperity,
To you and all your posterity.
And them that doesn't drink with sincerity,
That they may be damned for eternity!

>-+-0-+-<

May your neighbors respect you,
Trouble neglect you,
The angels protect you
And heaven accept you.

>-+-0-+-<

Mothers [fathers] hold their children's hands for just a
little while... And their hearts forever.

>-+-0-+-<

CHAPTER 11

INTERNATIONAL TOASTS

There are many ways in this world to say cheers. Although specific languages may have more extensive translation, the phrases we have included all basically mean cheers or some form of congratulations. If you choose to use an international toast, you might be wise to check out the exact pronunciation with someone from that country. Your goal is to appear worldly or generous for trying to involve yourself in another culture. You will be acting against your goal if your pronunciation turns cheers into "your mother has chicken feet."

>+⦿+<

Albanian: Gëzuar! ("All good things to you.")
Se hetan ("To your health.")

>+⦿+<

Arabic: Al salam alaycum. ("Peace be with you.")
B' ism Allah! ("In God's name.")
Fi sihtak! ("To your health.")
Kasak! ("In your honor.")

><+<>+O+<>+<

Armenian: Genatzt

><+<>+O+<>+<

Austrian: Prosit! ("May it be to your health.")

><+<>+O+<>+<

Belgian: Op uw gezonheid! ("To your health.")

><+<>+O+<>+<

Brazilian: Saúde! Viva! ("To your health.")

>-+-◊-◦-◊-+-<

Chinese: Yum sen! ("Drink to victory.")

>-+-◊-◦-◊-+-<

Czech/Slovak: Na Zdravi! ("Health to you.")

>-+-◊-◦-◊-+-<

Danish: Skal! ("A salute to you.")

>-+-◊-◦-◊-+-<

Dutch: Proost!
Geluch!

>-+-◊-◦-◊-+-<

Esperanto: Je zia sano!

>-+-•❀-•-O--•-❀-+-•-<

Estonian: Tervist! ("Good health to you.")

>-+-•❀-•-O--•-❀-+-•-<

Farsi: Salumati!

>-+-•❀-•-O--•-❀-+-•-<

Finnish: Kippis! Terveydeksi! ("To your health.")

>-+-•❀-•-O--•-❀-+-•-<

French: A vortre santé! Santé! Chin! ("To your health.")

>-+-•❀-•-O--•-❀-+-•-<

German: Prosit! ("To health.")

$\succ\!\!\cdot\!\!\bullet\!\!\cdot\!\!\circ\!\!\cdot\!\!\bullet\!\!\cdot\!\!\prec$

Greek: Eis Igian!

$\succ\!\!\cdot\!\!\bullet\!\!\cdot\!\!\circ\!\!\cdot\!\!\bullet\!\!\cdot\!\!\prec$

Greenlandic: Kasuguta!

$\succ\!\!\cdot\!\!\bullet\!\!\cdot\!\!\circ\!\!\cdot\!\!\bullet\!\!\cdot\!\!\prec$

Hawaiian: Havoli maoli oe! ("To your happiness.")

$\succ\!\!\cdot\!\!\bullet\!\!\cdot\!\!\circ\!\!\cdot\!\!\bullet\!\!\cdot\!\!\prec$

Hebrew: L'Chaim ("To life!")

$\succ\!\!\cdot\!\!\bullet\!\!\cdot\!\!\circ\!\!\cdot\!\!\bullet\!\!\cdot\!\!\prec$

Hungarian: Kedves egeszsegere!

Icelandic: Santanka nu!

Indian: Aap ki sehat ue liye! ("To your health.")

Indonesian: Selemat!

Irish: Slante!

Italian: A la salute!

Japanese: Omedeto Gozaimasu! ("Congratulations.")
Kampai! Banzai! Campi! ("Bottoms up.")

Korean: Gung bai! ("Bottoms up.")

Lithuanian: I sveikatas! ("To your health.")

Mexican: Salud!

Moroccan: Saha wa'afiab!

⊱——•○•——⊰

New Zealand: Kia ora!

⊱——•○•——⊰

Norwegian: Skal!

⊱——•○•——⊰

Pakistani: Sanda bashi!

⊱——•○•——⊰

Philippine: Mabuhay!

⊱——•○•——⊰

Polish: Na zdrowie! ("To your health.")
Sto lot! ("Another 100 years.")

＞┼╾＊＞━○━＜＊╼┼＜

Portuguese: A sua suade!

＞┼╾＊＞━○━＜＊╼┼＜

Romanian: Noroc! ("Good luck.")

＞┼╾＊＞━○━＜＊╼┼＜

Russian: Budem zdorovy! ("Let's be healthy!")
S priyezdom! ("Happy arrival!")
S otyezdom! ("Happy journey!")
Do dna! ("Bottom's up!")

＞┼╾＊＞━○━＜＊╼┼＜

Spanish: Salud!

＞┼╾＊＞━○━＜＊╼┼＜

Swedish: Skal!

>─┼─◦─┼─◦─┼─◦─┼─◄

Thai: Sawasdi!

>─┼─◦─┼─◦─┼─◦─┼─◄

Turkish: Serefe!

>─┼─◦─┼─◦─┼─◦─┼─◄

Ukranian: Na zdorovya! ("To your health!)

>─┼─◦─┼─◦─┼─◦─┼─◄

Welsh: Iechyd da!

>─┼─◦─┼─◦─┼─◦─┼─◄

Yiddish: Zol zon tzgezhint! ("To your good health.")

>—+—‹•›—O—‹•›—+—‹

Zulu: Oogy wawa!

>—+—‹•›—O—‹•›—+—‹

CHAPTER 12

ALL-OCCASION TOASTS

There are some toasts that do not fit neatly into any one category or at least we didn't agree on quite where to put them. If you find one you like, memorize it so you can impress someone at the spur of the moment. You never know when some additional charm might come in handy.

>—+—•••—O—•—+—<

*Let us toast the fools; but for them the rest of us could
not succeed.*
—Mark Twain (1835-1910)

>—+—•••—O—•—+—<

*Fill high the goblet! Envious time steals, as we speak,
our fleeting prime.*

>—+—•••—O—•—+—<

Toasts for All Occasions

Here's hoping that you live forever, and mine is the last voice you hear.

May our lives, like the leaves of the maple,
Grow more beautiful and fade.
May we say our farewells when it's time to go,
All smiling and unafraid.

May we keep a little of the fuel of youth to warm our body in old age.

May you enter Heaven late.

To the old, long life and treasure;
To the young, health and pleasure.

><del>+</del>O<del>+</del>><del></del>

Non corber indum illeitimie (Latin: "Don't let the
bastards get you down.")

><del>+</del>O<del>+</del>><del></del>

To better times and a speedy calm to the storms of life.

><del>+</del>O<del>+</del>><del></del>

All of this has been a religious experience: a living hell.

><del>+</del>O<del>+</del>><del></del>

Let us make the glasses kiss; let us quench the sorrow
ciders.

><del>+</del>O<del>+</del>><del></del>

Toasts for All Occasions

Come fill the bowl, each jolly soul;
Let Bacchus guide our revels;
Join the cup to lip, with "hip, hip, hip,"
And bury the blue devils.

>+‹+‹›+‹›+‹

Here's to thee my honest friend,
Wishing these hard times to mend.
Laugh and the world laughs with you;
Weep and it gives you the laugh anyway.

>+‹+‹›+‹›+‹

May poverty always be a day's march behind us.

>+‹+‹›+‹›+‹

May the morning of prosperity shine on the evening of
adversity.

>+‹+‹›+‹›+‹

May the sunshine of comfort dispel the clouds of despair.

>─┼─◉─◦─◖─┼─◄

May we ever be able to part with our troubles to advantage.

>─┼─◉─◦─◖─┼─◄

The right time and place is coming for you; don't let it pass.

>─┼─◉─◦─◖─┼─◄

Ad multos annos—to many years!

>─┼─◉─◦─◖─┼─◄

Toasts for All Occasions

A health to you,
A wealth to you,
And the best that life can give to you.

Here's to beefsteak when you're hungry,
Whiskey when you're dry,
Greenbacks when you're busted,
And Heaven when you die!

We'll think of all the friends we know,
And drink to all worth drinking to.

To all that gives you pleasure.

To blue skies and green lights.

>-+-#-+-O-+-#-+-<

Call frequently,
Drink moderately,
Park friendly,
Pay today, trust tomorrow.

>-+-#-+-O-+-#-+-<

To days of ease and nights of pleasure.

>-+-#-+-O-+-#-+-<

Delicious nights to an ever virtuous heart.

>-+-#-+-O-+-#-+-<

Good company, good wine, and good welcome make
good people.

>-+-#-+-O-+-#-+-<

Toasts for All Occasions

Good day, good health, good cheer, good night!

━━━◦━━

Here's to beauty, wit, and wine.

━━━◦━━

To a full stomach, a full purse, and a full heart.

━━━◦━━

I drink to the days that are.

━━━◦━━

It is best to rise from life as from the banquet, neither thirsty nor drunken.

━━━◦━━

Love to one, friendship to many.

><+<*>+-O+<*>+-<

May our faults be written on the seashore, and every good action prove a wave to wash them out.

><+<*>+-O+<*>+-<

May the clouds in your life form only a background for a lovely sunset.

><+<*>+-O+<*>+-<

May you have warmth in your igloo, oil in your lamp, and peace in your heart.

><+<*>+-O+<*>+-<

May we all live in pleasure and die out of debt.

><+<*>+-O+<*>+-<

May we be happy and our enemies know it.

May we live respected and die regretted.

May we live to learn well, and learn to live well.

May we never feel want, nor ever want feeling.

May you always distinguish between the weeds and the flowers.

May your life be as beautiful as a summer day, with just enough clouds to make you appreciate the sunshine.

Here's to the riotous enjoyment of quiet conscience.

'Tis hard to tell which is best;
Music, food, drink, or rest.

It's not so bad a world,
As some would like to make it;
But whether good or whether bad,
Depends on how you take it.

Toasts for All Occasions

Here's to our guest—
Don't let him rest.
But keep his elbow bending.
It's time to drink—
There's time to think,
Tomorrow—when you're mending.

>+-+⊕-+○-+⊕-+<

May our house always be too small to hold all our
friends.

>+-+⊕-+○-+⊕-+<

Stay happy, my friends, hang easy and loose,
Gettin' rattlesnake-riled is just no use.

>+-+⊕-+○-+⊕-+<

So here is a slogan that's sure to match,
There ain't no use itchin' unless you can scratch.

>+-+⊕-+○-+⊕-+<

The ornament of a house is the guests who frequent it.

><del>><del>><del>O><del>><del>><del><

Happy to share with you,
Such as we got,
The leaks in the roof
The soup in the pot.
You don't have to thank us,
Or laugh at our jokes,
Sit deep and come often,
You're one of the folks.

><del>><del>><del>O><del>><del>><del><

May love draw the curtain and friendship the cork.

><del>><del>><del>O><del>><del>><del><

Health and happiness!

><del>><del>><del>O><del>><del>><del><

Toasts for All Occasions

May all your troubles be little ones.

May all your days be as happy as the ones before.

Here's to you as good as you are,
Here's to me as bad as I am.
As bad as I am, as good as you are,
I'm as good as you are as bad as I am.

May your journey through life be guided by fair winds
and following seas.

A toast to the glorious mysteries of life.
To all that binds the family as one.
To mirth, merriment, mischief.
To dear friends, to youth,
To passion, to desire,
To pain, to tonight.

>+++0++<

May you pluck the feathers from the bird of life and may
they tickle your fancy!

>+++0++<

May your troubles be like grandma's teeth: few and far
between!

>+++0++<

May your boots never get dusty, and your guns never get
rusty.

>+++0++<

Health, love, money, and time to spend it.

>─┼─⊕─○─⊂⊦─◄

May all your pleasures become habits, and all your habits become legal.

>─┼─⊕─○─⊂⊦─◄

Here's to bread; it makes the best toast!

>─┼─⊕─○─⊂⊦─◄

Always walk with your faces toward the sun, so the shadows will fall behind you.

>─┼─⊕─○─⊂⊦─◄

Here's to every day that ends in "y."

>─┼─⊕─○─⊂⊦─◄

Here's to the roof above: May it never fall in, and may our friends gathered below it never fall out!

>−+‹›·O·‹›+−‹

To everyone everywhere: Be to your virtues a little kind, and your faults a little blind.

>−+‹›·O·‹›+−‹

Here's to my lips and here's to my toes, where many quarts and gallons goes!!

>−+‹›·O·‹›+−‹

May you have the hindsight to know where you have been, the foresight to know where you are going, and the insight to know when you have gone too far.

>−+‹›·O·‹›+−‹

Always walk with your faces to the sun, so the shadows will fall behind you.

>−+‹›·O·‹›+−‹

It's a reality of life that men are competitive. And the most competitive games draw the most competitive men. That's why they're there—to compete. They know the rules and the objectives when they get into the game. The objective is to win—fairly, squarely, decently, by the rules, but to win. And in truth, I've never known a man worth his salt who, in the long run, deep down in his heart, didn't appreciate the grind and the discipline. There is something in good men that really yearns for, that needs, that demands, discipline and the harsh reality of head to head combat. I don't say these things because I believe in the brute nature of man, nor that man must brutalize to be combative. I believe in God. I believe in human decency. But above all, I believe that any man's finest hour, his greatest fulfillment to all that he holds dear, is that moment when he has worked his heart out in a good cause and lies exhausted on the field of battle, victorious!
—Vince Lombardi, football coach

> ― + ∙● ∙ O ∙ ●+ ∙ ― ◄

We're only here for a short time, but we're here for a good time.

> ― + ∙● ∙ O ∙ ●+ ∙ ― ◄

To the chef: Good food, good meat, good God, let's eat!

> ― + ∙● ∙ O ∙ ●+ ∙ ― ◄

When there's love in the heart,
There will be beauty in the character.
When there is beauty in the character,
There will be harmony in the home.
When there is harmony in the home,
There will be order in the nation.
And when there is order in the nation,
There shall be peace in the world.
—Anonymous

Iron is strong, but fire melts it.
Fire is strong, but water quenches it.
Water is strong, but the sun evaporates it.
The sun is strong, but clouds can cover it.
Clouds are strong, but wind can drive clouds away.
Wind is strong, but man can shut it out.
Man is strong, but fears cast him down.
Fear is strong, but sleep overcomes it.
Sleep is strong, but death is stronger.
But the strongest is kindness.
It survives death.
—paraphrased from the Talmud

Bite off more than you can chew, then chew it.
Plan more than you can do, then do it.
Point your arrow at a star, take your aim and there you
are.
Arrange more time than you can spare, then spare it.
Take on more than you can bear, then bear it.
Plan your castle in the air, then build a ship to take you
there.
—Anonymous

>–+–◦–◦–◦–+–<

To laugh is to risk appearing the fool; laugh anyway.
To weep is to risk appearing sentimental; weep anyway.
To reach out for another is to risk involvement; get
involved anyway.
To place your ideas and dreams before a crowd is to risk
their loss; share your ideas anyway, and dream anyway.
To love is to risk being loved in return; risk love
anyway.
To live is to risk dying; risk living anyway.
To hope is to risk failure; you must have hope anyway.
But risks must be taken. The greatest hazard in life is to
risk nothing and do nothing—you will dull the spirit.
You may avoid suffering and sorrow, but cannot learn,
feel, change, grow, love, and live. Chained by your
attitude, you are a slave. You have forfeited freedom.
Only if you risk are you free.
—Anonymous

>–+–◦–◦–◦–+–<

Children Learn What They Live

If a child lives with criticism, he learns to condemn.
If a child lives with hostility, he learns to fight.
If a child lives with ridicule, he learns to be shy.
If a child lives with encouragement, he learns
confidence.
If a child lives with shame, he learns to feel guilty.
If a child lives with tolerance, he learns to be patient.
If a child lives with praise, he learns to appreciate.
—Anonymous

CHAPTER 13

FAMOUS CINEMA TOASTS

From recent Oscar-winners to old favorites, Hollywood films have been the source of some memorable toasts. Although you may discover some fitting sentiments here to add to your own toasts, we offer the following simply for your pleasure. As you can see, some of the finer moments of cinema have been of the toasting variety.

>—◆—○—◆—◄

To making it count.

—Leonardo Di Caprio, "Titanic"

>—◆—○—◆—◄

May the force be with you.

—Sir Alec Guiness, "Star Wars"

>—◆—○—◆—◄

Live long and prosper.

—Leonard Nimoy, "Star Trek"

Here's mud in your eye.

—The Three Stooges

Here's looking at you kid.

—Humphrey Bogart, "Casablanca"

Here's to plain speaking and clear understanding.

—Humphrey Bogart, "The Maltese Falcon"

Here's mud in my throat.

—Bob Hope, "Son of Paleface"

Early to rise and early to bed makes a man healthy but socially dead.

—Alan Hale, "They Drive by Night"

A toast a toast a toast to mother dollar and to papa dollar. And if you want to keep this old building and loan in business you'd better have a family real quick.

—James Stewart, "It's a Wonderful Life"

Here's to us, to apple trees, to cheese and wine and bread and life itself.

—Alan Alda, "The Four Seasons"

A toast—Jedediah—to life on my terms. These are the only terms anybody ever knows, his own.

—Orson Welles, "Citizen Kane"

Toasts for All Occasions

Here's to the time when we were little girls and no one asked us to marry.

—Joan Crawford, "Humoresque"

To the fountain of Trevi where hope can be found for a penny.

—Dorothy McGuire, "Three Coins in the Fountain"

Revenge is a dish that is best served cold.

—Ricardo Montalban, "Star Trek II: The Wrath of Khan"

To the men we loved: the stinkers.

—Eve Arden, "Mildred Pierce"

I keep my friends close but my enemies closer.

—Marlon Brando, "The Godfather"

I am sorry to drag you from your delicious dessert but there are one or two little things I feel I should say as best man. This is only the second time I've been a best man. I hope I did the job all right. At least the couple in question are still talking to me. They are not actually talking to each other. The divorce came through a couple of months ago. But I'm sure it had absolutely nothing to do with me. Apparently Paula knew that Peter had slept with her younger sister before I mentioned it in my speech. The fact that he slept with her mother came as a surprise. But I think it was incidental to the nightmare of recrimination and violence that became their two-day marriage.

But my job today is to talk about Angus and there are no skeletons in his cupboard.

I am ever in bewildered awe of anyone who makes this kind of commitment that (they) have made today. I know I couldn't do it.

—Hugh Grant, "Four Weddings and a Funeral"

CONCLUSION

Whether you prefer tea, beer, or champagne, the act of proposing a toast has little to do with beverage and everything to do with festivity. With a toast you can honor someone, congratulate them, roast them, and chide them. You can propose, dispose (retirement), or let off steam. You can wish people well or you can wish people hell. The best thing about the art of toasting is that you have room to use your own unique style within the boundaries of decency and what will most protect you from a punch in the mouth. In other words if you choose your words wisely you can be the life of the party. If you plan to use your forum to vent frustrations, insult, or bring attention to yourself at the expense of the honoree go back and read this book again.

We hope you were able to find the right toast for your occasion. If you have toasts you would like to share we would love to hear from you.

Here's to the readers of toasts who make our jobs worthwhile;
Here's to the givers of toasts who make their listeners
smile.
Here's to our book's publisher and editors who gave this
book a trial,
And here's to royalty checks, we hope we earn a pile.

WRITE A TOAST

These pages are for you to create your own special toasts. Although we have shown you examples of toasts for all occasions, you may have occasions we have yet to conceive. For that matter, the best toasts may have yet to be written. Who knows? Maybe the toast you write today will become the favorite saying of tomorrow. We know it will become a treasured memory for your family and friends to share.

_____

_____

_____

_____

_____

_____

_____

WRITE A TOAST

_____

_____

_____

_____

_____

_____

_____

_____

_____

_____

_____

_____

_____

_____

_____

_____

_____

_____

_____

_____

_____

_____

WRITE A TOAST

_____

_____

_____

_____

_____

_____

_____

_____

_____

_____

_____

_____

_____

_____

_____

_____

_____

_____

WRITE A TOAST